THE USBORNE SOCCER SCHOOL
BALL CONTROL

Gill Harvey

Designed by Stephen Wright
Edited by Cheryl Evans
Photographs by Chris Cole (Allsport UK)
Library photographs: Allsport UK

Illustrations by Bob Bond
Consultant: Phil Darren

With special thanks to Bobby Charlton International Ltd. for advice, soccer facilities
and soccer players: John Cox, Nathan Miles, Andrew Perkin, Leanne Prince, Ben
Tipton and Neil Wilson, and to their coach, Bryn Cooper

DTP by John Russell

CONTENTS

GETTING STARTED

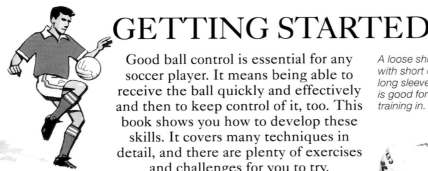

Good ball control is essential for any soccer player. It means being able to receive the ball quickly and effectively and then to keep control of it, too. This book shows you how to develop these skills. It covers many techniques in detail, and there are plenty of exercises and challenges for you to try.

A loose shirt with short or long sleeves is good for training in.

WHAT DO I NEED?

All you need to train with are a soccer ball and some markers. Special sports markers are shown in this book, but you can use bags or sweaters. Wear loose, comfortable clothing such as a tracksuit or shorts and T-shirt. On most surfaces trainers are fine, but soccer boots are best if you are playing on muddy ground.

Don't wear shorts or tracksuit bottoms that are tight. They will slow you down.

Shinpads protect you against hard tackles.

You will see markers like this throughout the book.

WARMING UP

To have good ball control, you need to be able to move your whole body well. Being able to twist, turn and keep your balance are key skills for many control techniques.

Do this exercise in pairs. More than one pair can play at once. It is a good warm-up exercise which will improve your balance and movement.

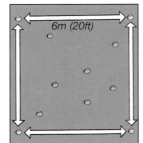

6m (20ft)

Mark out a 6m (20ft) square. Scatter six or seven markers inside it. Decide who will be attacker and who will be defender.

The attacker dribbles forward, weaving around the markers. The defender tries to stop him reaching the other side.

You cannot touch each other or leave the square. If the defender forces the attacker off the square, he has won.

GETTING THE FEEL OF THE BALL

If you are used to playing around with a soccer ball you will probably already have some idea of how the ball responds when you touch it in different ways. This is what it means to have a feel for the ball. This page looks more closely at how this works and how you can use the different parts of your foot to do different things.

This exercise helps you to get a feel for the parts of your foot that you use most often - the inside, outside and instep (see left).

Lay out seven markers 2m (6ft) apart in a zigzag line. Push the ball from the first to the second with the outside of your foot.

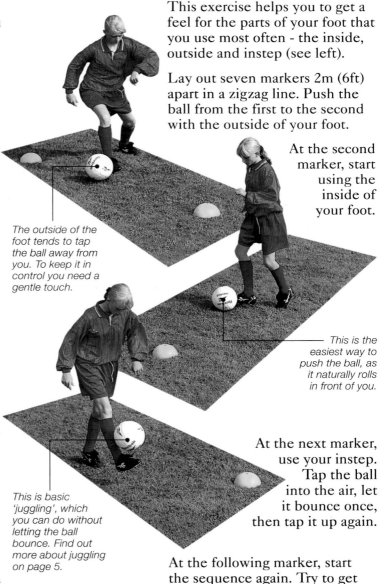

At the second marker, start using the inside of your foot.

The inside of your foot is used most often. Use it for controlling, dribbling and passing.

The outside of the foot tends to tap the ball away from you. To keep it in control you need a gentle touch.

The outside of your foot is useful for turning, dribbling and passing the ball to the side.

This is the easiest way to push the ball, as it naturally rolls in front of you.

Your instep is the most powerful part of your foot. It is best for kicking, especially shooting.

At the next marker, use your instep. Tap the ball into the air, let it bounce once, then tap it up again.

Your heel is not often used, but it is good for flicking the ball backwards or a quick reverse pass.

This is basic 'juggling', which you can do without letting the ball bounce. Find out more about juggling on page 5.

At the following marker, start the sequence again. Try to get used to using both your left and your right foot.

It is very difficult to control the ball with the tips of your toes. You should hardly ever use them.

CHALLENGE

When you see this trophy, you will find an idea for a challenge. Soccer is very competitive, so you need to keep pushing yourself to improve your personal best for every exercise. Get into the habit of giving yourself new targets each time you practise so that you can tell how fast your skills are growing.

It is risky to use the sole of your foot to control the ball, but you use it for some trick moves.

MOVING ON

Once you have a basic feel for the ball you are on the way to developing good control. The next stage is to do plenty of practice to develop your skills. Things like juggling the ball are good for this, but you also need to work on special control methods. Here you can find out about the basic techniques that will help you.

JUGGLING

Although you rarely use juggling in an actual game, it helps you to develop the quick reactions, tight ball control and concentration that you need in order to play well.

To get the ball into the air, roll your foot back over the top of the ball, then hook it under and flick the ball up.

Keep the ball in the air by bouncing it off your foot. Hold your foot out flat. If you point your toes up, you will probably lose control.

As you develop your control, pass from one foot to the other, or bounce it up further into the air so that you juggle it on your knee.

Keep your eye on the ball all the time.

You could try juggling the ball on your shoulder and with your head.

JUGGLING GAME

Work on your juggling with a group of friends. Choose someone to be a caller. All of you dribble until the caller shouts 'Up!'

Everyone flicks the ball up and juggles. The last one to keep the ball in the air wins. When he drops it, you all start dribbling again.

RECEIVING THE BALL

Controlling the ball as you receive it is one of the most important skills you can learn. Everything else you do depends on this, so it's well worth spending plenty of time on it. These are the main points to remember.

1. To get your timing right, you need to judge the flight of the ball carefully.

2. Don't just hope the ball will come straight to you. Move into line with it.

3. Decide early which part of your body you will use to control the ball.

4. Once you have the ball, don't hesitate. Decide on your next move quickly.

FIRST TOUCH

This player is demonstrating good first touch. The ball is moving and in a good position to be played away.

The moment you make contact with the ball is called the 'first touch.' A good first touch keeps the ball moving and places it a short distance from your feet. To develop this skill, you need to 'cushion' the ball.

WHAT IS CUSHIONING?

Cushioning means taking the speed out of the ball, just as a cushion would if it was attached to your body. It slows the ball down without making it bounce away. Here you can see how cushioning works in practice.

As the ball travels toward you, position your foot in line with it to receive it.

On making contact, relax your foot and let it travel back with the ball.

The speed of the ball is absorbed. It slows down and you can play it away.

5

FOOT CONTROL

Your feet are the parts of your body that you use most often to receive the ball. Remember that a good first touch keeps the ball moving, so use the inside, outside or instep of your foot rather than your sole. Try to slow the ball down and position it in one smooth movement.

USING THE INSIDE OF YOUR FOOT

If you use the inside of your foot, you will be in a good position to play the ball away when you have cushioned it.

This player is balanced and in line with the ball.

Watch the ball as it approaches and place your foot in line with it. Balance on one leg with your receiving foot turned out.

As you receive the ball with the inside of your foot, relax your leg and foot so that they travel back with it.

The ball should drop just in front of your feet. Look around you and play it away to the left or right as quickly as possible.

Make sure you work on receiving with your left and your right foot.

USING THE OUTSIDE OF YOUR FOOT

If you are going to use the outside of your foot, decide to do so quickly and turn so that your side faces the ball.

Lift your leg to receive the ball with the outside of your foot. Relax your foot back and down to the ground.

Push the ball to the outside with the same foot, as you can see here, or across your body with either foot.

USING YOUR INSTEP

To control the ball with your instep, make sure you are facing the ball with your arms out for balance.

Lift your foot, but keep it flat. If you point your toes up the ball will probably bounce off them.

Just as you receive the ball, lower your foot to the ground, letting the ball drop off it in front of you.

THINGS TO AVOID

Try not to stop the ball dead. If you do, you have to touch it again before you can play your next move.

If the ball bounces off your foot and ends up a long way from you, you waste time chasing it.

PASS AND CONTROL EXERCISE

Do this exercise with a friend. Make a 'gate' with two markers and stand with the gate between you. Pass the ball through the gate so that your partner has to control it.

He turns and passes the ball down the outside of the gate. Control it, turn and pass it back through the gate or down the other side of it. Carry on passing and receiving like this.

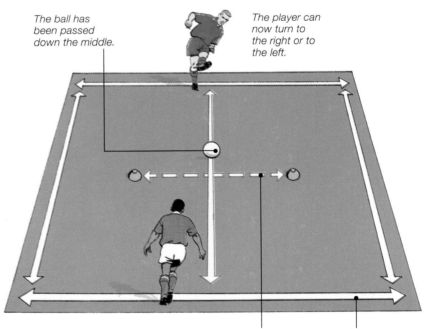

The ball has been passed down the middle.

The player can now turn to the right or to the left.

Try to vary your passes as much as possible, but keep them low.

Anticipate which way the ball will come and run for it.

The gate is about 2m (6ft) wide.

Your pitch is about 5m (15ft) wide.

HIGHER BALLS

When a ball comes at you from a higher angle, there are several things you can do. Depending on where you position yourself and how high the ball is, you can receive it with your foot, thigh or chest. Whichever you decide upon, you still use a cushioning technique to take the pace out of the ball.

USING YOUR THIGH

If you cushion the ball properly it shouldn't sting your leg.

Watch the ball carefully so that you can judge where it will land.

Bend your knee to meet the ball, using your arms for balance. On making contact, straighten your leg gradually so that the ball drops off your thigh in front of your feet.

USING YOUR FOOT

Keeping your arms out for balance, lift your leg to meet the ball. Catch it with the inside of your foot.

Without hooking your foot completely under the ball, drop it down to the ground, dragging the ball down with it.

USING YOUR CHEST

Your chest is good for cushioning because it is bigger than any other part of your body. Keep your hands open, because clenching your fist makes your chest muscles tighten and they need to relax. Keep your arms out of the way, too, to avoid handling the ball.

Put your arms back and open up your chest as the ball approaches you.

As the ball makes contact with you, cushion it by letting yourself relax.

Bring your shoulders in and hollow your chest, so that the ball rolls off you.

The ball drops to the ground gently and you are able to play your next move.

HIGH BALL PRACTICE

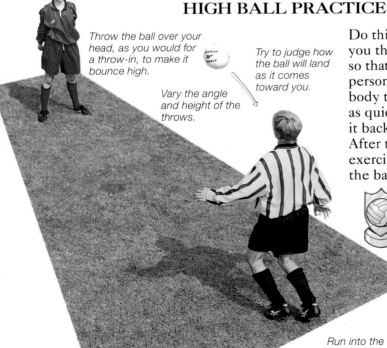

Throw the ball over your head, as you would for a throw-in, to make it bounce high.

Try to judge how the ball will land as it comes toward you.

Vary the angle and height of the throws.

Run into the best position to receive the ball.

Do this practice in pairs. One of you throws the ball to the other so that it bounces once. The other person decides which part of the body to control it with, controls it as quickly as possible and passes it back. Swap after ten throws. After ten throws each, repeat the exercise, this time without letting the ball bounce.

CHALLENGE

When you are doing the high ball practice, build up to controlling at least eight out of ten throws with no more than three touches. When both you and your partner can do this, compete with each other. Score out of ten.

HEADING THE BALL

Controlling the ball with your head is not very easy until you are sure of your heading technique, so these pages show you how to develop a range of heading skills. The main points to remember are to keep your eyes open and to use your forehead, not the top of your head. You may find it easier to begin with a fairly light, soft ball.

BASIC HEADING TECHNIQUE

Put yourself in line with the ball. With one foot in front of the other, bend your knees and lean back.

As the ball comes close, try to keep your eyes open. Stay relaxed right up to the last minute.

Attack the ball with your forehead. If you use any other part of your head it can be painful.

Push the ball away, keeping your neck muscles firm so that your head can direct the ball.

POWER HEADING

Put one foot in front of the other for balance and bend your legs as the ball comes toward you.

Keep your eyes fixed on the ball and take off on one foot. This gives you more power and height.

Drive forward as powerfully as you can with your forehead, keeping your eyes open.

Watch where the ball goes as you land so that you are ready to carry out your next move.

CONTROL HEADING

Use a control header to cushion the ball if you want to play the next move yourself instead of passing.

Don't lean quite as far back as the ball approaches. Stay relaxed to provide a cushion for the ball.

Hold your position as you receive the ball. Bend your knees and lean back slightly further.

Push the ball forward gently, so that it drops and lands not far from your feet.

HEADING PRACTICE

Work with a partner. Stand about 4m (12ft) apart. Your partner throws the ball for you to head back. Have five goes at each of these techniques, then swap.

First, cushion the ball with a control header. Let it drop to the ground. Pass it back.

Next, head the ball so that your partner can catch it easily.

Finally, power the ball away, heading it over your partner.

CHALLENGE

Set distance targets. For power headers, try to head the ball more than 6m (20ft). For control headers, try to head it no more than 1m (3ft) from your feet.

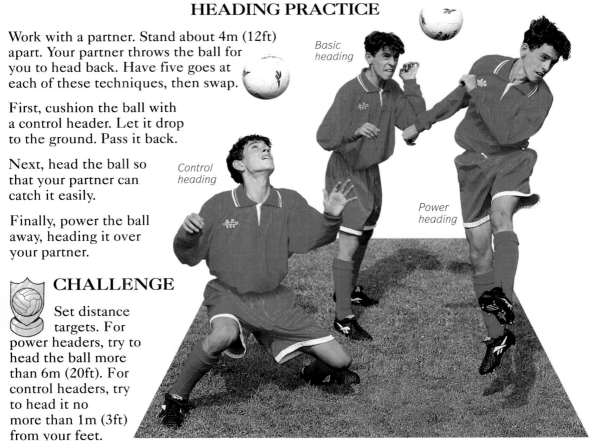

Basic heading

Control heading

Power heading

TURNING

Once you have received the ball and controlled it, you need to move off with it as fast as possible before an opponent can challenge you. You improve your chances of doing this effectively if you can turn quickly and sharply, so it is worth learning several turns to outwit your opponents.

Marker

TURNING 'OFF-LINE'

When you receive the ball, always try to turn immediately and take it off in another direction. This is what is meant by taking the ball 'off-line'. If you keep running in the same direction, it is too easy for your opponents to guess where the ball will go next. They will quickly be able to reach you and tackle you.

The ball has been passed to a player who is being closely marked.

This line shows the 'on-line' route that the player must try to avoid taking.

Instead of taking the on-line route, the player reaches the ball and turns off-line.

DOING AN INSIDE HOOK

As you receive the ball, watch out for approaching opponents and lean in the direction you want to go.

Drop your shoulder so that you are partly turned. Hook the inside of your foot around the ball.

Move off at a sharp angle, dragging the ball around with the inside of your foot. Accelerate away.

DOING AN OUTSIDE HOOK

To begin the turn, reach across your body and hook the ball at the bottom with the outside of your foot.

Sweep the ball around to the side with the same foot. Lean in the direction you want to go.

Turn to follow the path of the ball and accelerate away from your opponent as quickly as possible.

CONTROL AND TURNING EXERCISE

This exercise helps you to develop the different skills of controlling the ball and turning with it into one smooth movement. You will need three or more people.

1. Mark out a circle 10m (30ft) wide. Number the players. The highest (Player 4 here) has the ball and the lowest stands in the middle.

2. Player 4 begins the game by passing the ball into the middle. Player 1 controls it and turns with it. He can turn in any direction.

 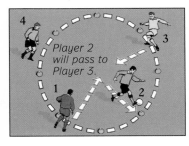

Player 2 will pass to Player 3.

3. Player 1 dribbles the ball to the edge of the circle and Player 2 runs to the middle. Player 1 turns and passes the ball back to Player 2.

4. Player 2 controls the ball, turns and runs to the edge. Player 3 takes his place in the middle. After Player 3, Player 4 runs in, and so on.

STAR TURN

Here, Swiss player Georges Bregy uses an inside hook to pull the ball away from Leonel Alvarez (Columbia).

CHALLENGE

Touching the ball lots of times slows you down, so try to touch it as little as possible. Count the number of touches you need to control the ball and turn it, then reduce this number to four or less.

TURNING TRICKS

Basic turns are useful for speed, but they do not disguise your movements very much. In many situations, a slightly more complicated turn can help you to fool your opponents. Be flexible, and experiment. You may prefer to develop your own way of doing a particular turn.

THE DRAG BACK TURN

This turn is ideal if you are being closely marked. Once you have mastered it, you can adapt it, depending on your position or that of your opponent.

Think about where to go next.

1. Draw your leg back as if you are about to kick the ball, but swing your foot over it instead.

2. As you bring your leg back again, catch the top of the ball with your foot and drag it back.

Spin quickly on your standing foot.

3. As you drag back, begin to spin on your other foot. Lean in the direction you want to go.

4. When you have pulled the ball all the way back, complete the turn. Accelerate past your opponent.

VARIATIONS

Instead of dragging the ball back, step to the inside. Push it away with the outside of your foot.

You can also step to the outside of the ball. Turn, pushing the ball with the inside of your foot.

THE CRUYFF TURN

This turn was named after the Dutch player Johan Cruyff. Try to exaggerate the movements. You can give the turn extra disguise by pretending to kick the ball first.

As you are about to do the turn, swing one foot around the ball so that it is in front of it. Keep this foot firmly on the ground.

Leaning away from the ball, push it back and then behind you with the other foot. Turn quickly and follow the ball.

Try to develop a quick flick of your foot to push the ball around.

Watch where the ball goes so that you can follow it.

TURNING PRACTICE

Work with a partner. Place four markers in the pattern shown and stand at the end ones. One person is the leader and the other person mirrors what he does.

Both dribble to the middle. Just before the marker, the leader turns. The other tries to mirror his turn.

Run out to the side marker, round it and back to the end ones. Try not to bump into each other as you cross.

Start toward the middle again and turn at the marker. The leader will now be the other player.

CHALLENGE

Compete with each other. Score a point for mirroring a turn correctly, or for fooling your opponent with a turn. Race back to your markers and score a point for winning. The first to ten points wins.

DRIBBLING

Once you have possession of the ball, you may want to pass or shoot, but one of the most exciting parts of playing soccer is keeping the ball under your control and dribbling it up the field. If you watch a good dribbler, the ball seems almost stuck to his feet as he runs. This is what you should aim for.

BASIC TECHNIQUE

You can use your instep to dribble, especially for the first few touches. Be careful not to kick the ball very far.

You are free to run faster if you use the outside of your foot, but try not to tap the ball too far out to the side.

The inside of your foot may feel the most comfortable to use.

Be careful not to let the ball get under your feet.

MOVEMENT AND BALANCE

You need to be flexible and balanced to dribble well. To develop these skills, dribble around a slalom. Lay ten markers about 4m (13ft) apart in a zigzag line. Start to dribble down the line, weaving around the markers.

4m (13ft)

Try dribbling with different parts of your feet to see which feels most comfortable.

Keep the ball close to your feet. Try to exaggerate the twists and turns, leaning as far as you can as you run.

Keep as close to the path of the slalom as possible. Turn sharply at the markers.

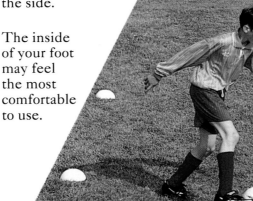

In a game, you would need to look out for other players, so try to look around as you dribble.

Gradually increase your speed. If you find that you cannot lean as far, slow down again until you improve.

Try to run lightly on your toes, so that you can change direction quickly and easily.

TAG DRIBBLE

This game is for up to four people, though more people can play if you make the square bigger.

1. Lay out a 6 x 6m (20 x 20ft) square with four markers. Each player has a ball and stands in the square.

2. Dribble around the square. Try to 'tag' other players without being tagged yourself and without losing control of the ball.

3. Keep a score. You gain a point each time you tag someone, and if you are tagged, you lose a point.

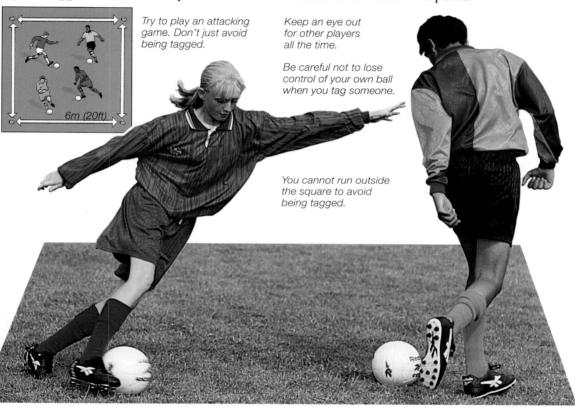

Try to play an attacking game. Don't just avoid being tagged.

6m (20ft)

Keep an eye out for other players all the time.

Be careful not to lose control of your own ball when you tag someone.

You cannot run outside the square to avoid being tagged.

IDEAL TECHNIQUE

Good dribbling should combine tight control with freedom of movement. Some people think that you should dribble with the outside of your foot as much as possible, because it gives you freedom to run and makes it easier for you to turn to the outside.

Here you can see Roberto Baggio of Italy dribbling with the ball at an ideal distance from his feet.

CHALLENGE

The best way to measure how you improve at dribbling is by timing yourself. When you dribble down a slalom, time yourself, then try to beat your record. Try to keep the ball close to your feet. Remember that there is no point in going faster unless the ball is under your control.

WORKING ON PACE

One of the things which will make your dribbling skills
more effective is being able to vary your speed. If you can
slow down or sprint away suddenly without losing control
of the ball, you add disguise to your game and increase
your chances of keeping possession.

CHANGES OF PACE

*Keep an eye out
for opponents
and opportunities
to pass.*

*Take long
strides so that
you cover as
much ground
as possible.*

*Be ready to slow
down and do
something different
if someone
challenges you.*

1. Fool opponents by
slowing down. This
gives you time to
take them by surprise.

2. To dodge around
someone, watch for
an opportunity to
change pace suddenly.

*Use the outside of
your foot to push
the ball forward
with little taps.*

3. Sprint as fast as
possible when you
have just dodged
around your opponent.

4. When you are clear
of opponents, choose
the pace that gives
you most control.

RUNNING WITH THE BALL

Running with the ball is
different from dribbling. It
means sprinting up the field
with a clear path ahead,
pushing the ball quite a
long way in front of you.
When you dribble you
keep the ball under
closer control, beating
opponents as you go.

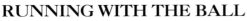
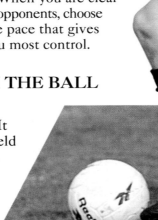

SLALOM AND SPRINT

You can play this with as many people as you like. You each need a ball. Lay down ten markers in a zig-zag line (see page 14), then place an extra marker 10m (30ft) from the last one. Make one course like this for each person.

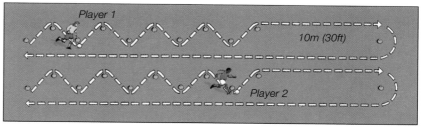

Player 1

10m (30ft)

Player 2

At the shout of 'Go!', everyone starts to dribble in and out of the slalom.

At the end of the slalom, accelerate. Run with the ball to the last marker.

Turn, then race back to the starting point with the ball. The first one back wins.

SPRINT AND STOP GAME

This game is for three or more players. Lay out a circle about 3m (10ft) wide and a bigger circle around it. There should be about 10m (30ft) between them. All of you begin to dribble around the inside circle.

Take turns shouting 'Go!' The player who shouts has an unfair advantage, so he cannot be the winner of that game.

To keep the ball close to the circle, use the outside of your foot. Brush the ball along with the foot nearest the circle.

This player has reached the outer circle and stopped with his foot on the ball, so he wins.

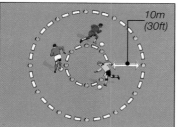

10m (30ft)

On the shout of 'Go!', turn and sprint out from the circle. The first person to reach the outer circle and put a foot on their ball is the winner. Dribble back to the inner circle and start the game again.

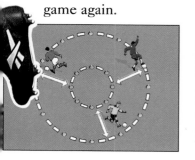

FEINTING

Feinting means fooling your opponents while you are dribbling. It is also called 'selling a dummy'. Two things will make your opponent move in a particular direction, either the movement of your body or the movement of the ball. Feinting uses the movement of your body.

A SIMPLE DUMMY

The simplest dummy or feint is pretending to go one way, then swerving and going the other. Here, Player 1 dribbles up the field as Player 2 comes to challenge him.

Player 1

Player 2

Player 1 drops his right shoulder, making Player 2 think that he is going to turn to the right.

Player 2 moves to the right, but Player 1 now swerves back to the left. He dodges around Player 2 and accelerates past him.

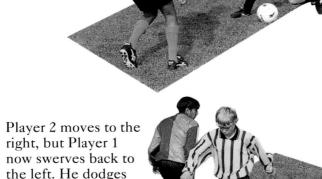

KEY FACTORS

Exaggerate your dropped shoulder and body swerve to fool your opponent.

Accelerate past your opponent before he has time to recover.

Be confident when you try to sell a dummy, or you risk losing the ball.

A STAR FEINT

Here, Alberto Garcia Aspe of Mexico drops his shoulder to sell a dummy to Paul McGrath of Ireland.

BASIC FEINTING PRACTICE

Work with a partner. Try to dribble past him, using a feint - you are not allowed to just push the ball past him and run.

If you get past him, turn and try again. If you don't, he dribbles past you instead. Score a point each time you get past.

GUESS AND DODGE GAME

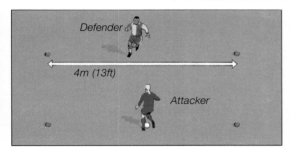

Defender

4m (13ft)

Attacker

The attacker here dodges to the left.

This makes the defender also turn to the left.

1. This is a game for two people with one ball. Both of you stand between two markers placed about 4m (13ft) apart.

2. Decide who will attack and who will defend. The attacker has the ball. The aim is for the attacker to reach a marker.

3. If the defender has his foot on one marker, the attacker has to go the other way. He cannot touch the matching marker.

4. Keep on playing until the attacker reaches a marker, then swap over so that you both have a turn at being attacker.

A good defender tries to watch the ball, not your movements. This game helps you to develop the speed and anticipation you need to beat him.

You need to be able to switch your balance from one foot to the other.

Once you see that your opponent is off balance, run for your marker quickly.

Here, the attacker has quickly turned to the right to reach the other marker.

FEINTING TRICKS

If you are trying to sell a dummy while you are dribbling, you stand a better chance of succeeding if you know a few trick moves. On these pages there are different ways to change direction and unbalance your opponent, which you can use as part of your feinting technique.

THE STOP MOVE

1. This move relies on a change of pace. Use it if someone is chasing you.

2. Accelerate slightly. As your opponent speeds up to follow, stop suddenly.

3. You should now be in a good position to use a drag back turn (see page 14).

4. You will be able to carry out the turn while your opponent is still off balance.

5. Finish the turn and start to move away at right angles to your original direction.

6. Your opponent is now facing the wrong way to chase you as you speed off.

THE STOP-START GAME

20m (60ft)

Work with a partner. Mark out a line about 20m (60ft) long. Dribble along it with your partner behind you.

Your partner can come alongside, but he cannot overtake you. Try to 'lose' him by stopping suddenly.

Your partner is thrown off balance.

You may confuse him more if you pretend to stop, then accelerate. Keep the ball on the side farthest from him.

CHALLENGE

Allow tackling in the stop-start game. Overtaking and sliding tackles are not allowed, but you can try to hook the ball away from the side. Score a point each time you succeed.

THE ZIGZAG MOVE

Try to exaggerate the move.

You don't need to rush.

1. Drop your shoulder and lean left to make it look as though you will push the ball across your body that way.

2. As your opponent gets closer, "show" him the ball. This confuses him into thinking he can intercept it.

You can reverse this move and turn to the left.

3. Just before he tries to tackle you, slide your right foot around the ball and hook it with the outside of your foot.

4. Pull the ball away to the right and push it past your opponent. Turn to follow it quickly and accelerate away.

SOLO PRACTICE

To gain confidence in using these moves, try doing them on your own with a marker. Pretend the marker is one of your opponents and dodge past it when you get close to it. Try using different moves.

THE SCISSORS MOVE

Dribble forward with the outside of your right foot. Make it look as though you will swerve out to the right.

Lift your foot suddenly and swing it around the front of the ball, taking a big stride as you do so.

Hook the outside of your other foot around the ball. Push it away as fast as you can to the left.

SHIELDING THE BALL

Shielding is a way of keeping control of the ball by preventing other players from getting at it. It is also known as 'screening'. You position yourself so that you become a shield between your opponent and the ball. Try to develop the habit of shielding whenever an opponent challenges you.

HOW TO SHIELD

The challenger risks giving away a foul if he tries to kick the ball from behind. He is more likely to kick you accidentally instead.

As soon as you are challenged, turn so that you are between the ball and your opponent.

Keep the ball close to your feet.

The challenger has to try to get in front of you. This gives you time to pass the ball or accelerate away.

The ball is now protected. Your opponent can only reach it from behind.

SHIELDING WHILE YOU ARE RUNNING

When you are running with the ball or dribbling, keep your head up to watch out for opponents coming up on your left or right side.

Be ready to change your body position from one side of the ball to the other. For example, if someone is coming up on the right, keep the ball on your left side.

IMPEDING OTHER PLAYERS

One of the laws of football is that you cannot 'impede the progress' of another player. This means that you cannot stop someone from reaching the ball unless you can play it yourself, or shield another player from the ball while you are still running for it. You cannot push or hold anyone either, so be careful to use your arms only as a shield.

This player is not breaking the rules, as he has possession of the ball. He is using his body and arms as a shield, but he is not holding or pushing the other player.

Here, the player is impeding. He has not yet reached the ball and is holding the other player back. He is also pushing with his arms, which is not allowed.

A STAR SHIELDING

Some players are known for shielding the ball more than others. It is important not to be afraid of making physical contact while you are playing, but this is never an excuse for giving away a foul.

Here you can see Dutch player Dennis Bergkamp using his arms and body correctly to shield the ball from an opponent.

TRUCK AND TRAILER

The trailer is not allowed to tackle.

Play this game in pairs. The player with the ball is the 'truck'. The other is the 'trailer'. The truck dribbles the ball while the trailer tries to get in front of him.

The truck has to twist and turn so that he is always shielding the ball. When the trailer gets in front of the truck, he becomes the truck instead.

CHALLENGE

When you are the trailer, make a real effort to dodge around the truck. If you are the truck, aim to protect the ball successfully for at least one minute before losing control of it.

TRICKS FOR FUN

Learning tricks can give your game a lot of extra flair and disguise. Some of the tricks on these pages are just for fun but others add an extra element to your control and dribbling skills, too. Learning any of them is worth the effort because you are still improving your control of the ball.

THE BEARDSLEY TRICK

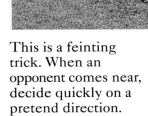

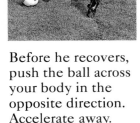

This is a feinting trick. When an opponent comes near, decide quickly on a pretend direction.

Lift your knee in the pretend direction. Really exaggerate the twist of your hips and body.

Your opponent will probably start to go the wrong way. Quickly bring your knee back down.

Before he recovers, push the ball across your body in the opposite direction. Accelerate away.

THE MARADONA MOVE

This move is sure to confuse your opponent. As the ball rolls toward you, step on it to stop it.

Step off the ball again, taking a big stride around it so that you begin to turn around the ball.

Finish turning so that your back is facing the direction you want to go. Put your other foot on top of the ball.

Drag the ball back behind you and quickly spin around again to follow it. Accelerate away.

THE FLICK OVER

This juggling trick is very spectacular, but don't use it in a game because you are almost certain to give the ball away to the other team. Learn it for fun and compete with your friends to see who can flick it highest.

You can try flicking the ball out to the side rather than over you.

Try not to look round at the ball as you do the flick.

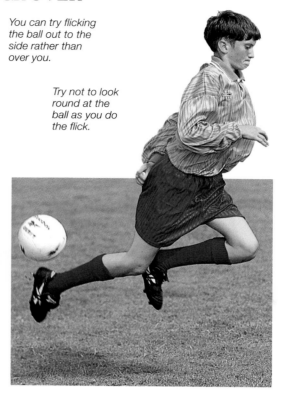

Step in front of the ball with one foot. Trap the ball between the toes of one foot and the heel of your other foot.

Roll the ball up your heel, then flick up backwards with your front foot as hard and high as you can so that it goes over you.

THE HEEL CATCH

This is another trick to try while you are juggling. Move in front of the ball, then lean forward and flick your heel up to catch it.

The ball should come round to the front of you again. Spin round to play it back into the air with your instep or knee.

THE NUTMEG

To nutmeg someone you push the ball between his legs. Don't try it unless his legs are far apart. Watch your opponent carefully and time it for when he least expects it. You can then run around him to collect the ball.

PLAYING IN A TEAM

As you build up your control skills, you will find it gradually easier to put them into practice when you are playing in matches. However, when you are playing in a team you need to think carefully about how to make the best use of your skills. Always think of the whole team, not just your own game.

KEEPING POSSESSION

Once your team has possession of the ball, it can control the whole game and create opportunities to score. Whatever you do, you should be helping your team to keep possession. You can do this by remembering these things:

Supporting player

This player is creating a chance to pass.

This player is marking a defender.

This player can see he is in a good position to dribble.

Support your team-mates by backing them up. Let them know you are there by calling to them.

Think ahead. Run into space so that other players can pass to you, or mark an opponent.

If someone passes to you, take the initiative and run for the ball. Don't wait for it to come to you.

When you receive the ball, look around to decide what to do next, then do it as quickly as possible.

DIRECTION

Change direction before opponents can reach you.

This player is passing the ball for his team member to collect.

To support another player, run into space so that he can pass forward to you.

When you are dribbling, it is fine to change direction as long as you are still moving up the field.

If you are being forced to turn back on yourself, you risk wasting time and space. Pass the ball instead.

If you need to pass the ball out of danger, try to pass it forward. Only pass back if you really have to.

WHEN TO DRIBBLE

When you receive the ball, check
to see if you are in a good
position to dribble. If you are
heavily marked but one of
your team-mates is free, it
makes more sense to
pass to him. If you
try to dribble, you
will probably
lose possession.

This player is in a better position to play the ball.

Dribbling is safest when the ball
is in your opponents' half of the
field. Never try to dribble
out of your own penalty
area, because it is far
too risky. Get the ball
out of the danger
area quickly by
passing it up
the field
instead.

TEAM DUMMIES

Here, the player with the ball can see a supporting player to his right as he dribbles up the field.

When you are dribbling,
keep your head up and
watch out for other players
who are moving with you
to give you support.

The player with the ball sells his opponent a dummy and pretends to pass to the right.

When you sell a dummy,
pretend to pass to a
member of your team.
This will make your
dummy more realistic.

As the player with the ball dodges round his opponent, the supporting player moves up with him.

You still have support, so
be ready to make
a real pass if you come
under too much pressure.

IMPROVING YOUR GAME

To keep on improving, you can play games which develop particular skills. Here, one game helps you to concentrate on your control and the other on your dribbling skills. Try to remember everything you have learned and put it into practice as you play.

TWO TOUCH

'Two touch' is an excellent game for improving your first touch of the ball. It also improves your anticipation, as you have to run into space to play it well.

Make things difficult for the other team by marking closely.

Control the ball with your first touch and pass it with your second.

Mark out a pitch and two goals. Divide into teams. Play as you would in a normal game, but each player is only allowed to touch the ball twice before another player touches it.

If a player makes a third touch, the ball passes to the other team.

Try this variation if there are five or less of you. Play with just one goal, so that the goalkeeper opposes both teams.
 To keep the game moving fast, pass as much as possible before shooting.

REMINDER TIPS

★ Look for space and run into it, so that other players can pass to you.

★ Don't just hope the ball will come directly to you. Run to meet it.

★ Watch the flight of the ball carefully. Get in line with it to receive it.

★ Decide quickly which part of the body you will use to control the ball.

★ Cushion the ball with as few touches as possible. Try to cushion with your first touch.

★ Play your next move quickly before an opponent can reach you.

PINBALL DRIBBLE

This game will help you with your dribbling, feinting and shielding skills. Lay out a line of boxes, one for each person playing. In the game shown there are four.

If you find it difficult to get past a particular player, try something different each time you have to pass him.

If the ball goes out of the box, this counts as losing it and the player goes into the second box.

The player in the first box tries to dribble through the next box. The player there tries to tackle him.

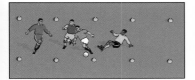

If he gets through this box, he scores a point and moves on. He scores a point for each box he dribbles through.

When he loses the ball or gets to the end, he goes into the second box. Everyone else moves back a box.

The player in the last box runs to the first and starts to dribble. Continue playing like this, keeping a note of each player's score. The first person to score five points is the winner.

REMINDER TIPS

★ Keep your head up so that you can see what your opponent is doing.

★ Keep the ball close to you as you dribble, using different parts of your feet.

★ Drop your shoulder and make use of body swerve to trick your opponent.

★ Try out different trick moves and feints to unbalance your opponent.

★ Keep your body between the ball and your opponent to shield it from him.

★ Accelerate away from opponents as fast as you can.

INDEX

If you would like to improve your soccer by
attending a soccer course in your holidays, you
can find out about different courses from:

Bobby Charlton International Ltd
Hopwood Hall
Rochdale Rd
Middleton
Manchester M24 6XH
Tel: 0161 643 3113

First published in 1996 by Usborne Publishing
Ltd, 83-85 Saffron Hill, London EC1N 8RT,
England.
Copyright © 1996 Usborne Publishing Ltd.

THE USBORNE
SOCCER SCHOOL